C# - Learn by coding your own popular game

INDEX

Introduction 4

Special Offer 4

About C# 6

What you will need 8

Module - 1: Flabby Bird 12

Module - 2: Code 15

Module - 3: Make it your own 38

Module - 4: Engines and APIs 41

Module - 5: Conclusion 43

More book from William

https://www.amazon.com/dp/B071X9RGP5 (2.99$ Ebook)

Introduction

Special Offer

You probably bought this book to learn more about programming in C# and make of it your work later, or to learn C# and build up your own personal project. Whatever the reason, you have chosen this book and I thank you greatly.

Now I have a more than special offer to let you know! Imagine yourself learning C# programming from A to Z, acquiring the necessary knowledge to work in this field? Achieve all your goals and projects completely free? Yes, yes, for free! This is not a scam : let me explain to you. Amazon works in the following way; To increase the number of buyers and feedbacks, Amazon grants a promotion that allows, for a certain number of days, to have some books for free. Do you see what I mean? Imagine yourself getting ALL C#, C, C++ books and more again for free! Learn how to code without having to spend a single penny! Moreover, it has never been easier to join my Email list (Click the following link) : https://williamrothschild.lpages.co/william-s-rothschild/ . You will automatically receive a confirmation email, because I want to be certain that you are interested. Do not worry, I will NOT send any spam and will not disclose your personal information to anyone.

With your email address, I intend to share with you the dates when my books will be published AS WELL AS the dates when my books will be free. Also, I will share with you articles, update and useful informations to help you in your programming journey, and much more. Only individuals who have subscribed to my Email list will be able to benefit from this valuable information. Thanks you and see you soon!

About C#

This book will cover how to build a simple Flappy bird game. From the instance of starting up your coding platform up to building it and compiling it. This book was written using C# in Visual Basic, so any other platforms might possess more or less of the options availed.

C# is a simple, modern, general-purpose, object-oriented programming language developed by Microsoft. C# programming is very much based on C and C++ programming languages, so if you have a basic understanding of C or C++ programming, then it will be fun to learn C#.

C# is designed for Common Language Infrastructure (CLI), which consists of the executable code and runtime environment that allows use of various high-level languages on different computer platforms and architectures.

The following reasons make C# a widely used professional language:

- It is a modern, general-purpose programming language

- It is object oriented.

- It is component oriented.

- It is easy to learn.

- It is a structured language.

- It produces efficient programs.

- It can be compiled on a variety of computer platforms.

- It is a part of .Net Framework.

Without any further ado, let's get started!

What you will need

You will need to start Visual Studio (you don't say)! On the menu bar, choose File -> New -> Project, and the New Project dialog box will open. This dialog box lists the different default application types that Visual C# can create. Expand Installed, expand Templates, expand Visual C#, and then choose Windows Forms Application. Choose the name you want for your game and click Ok.

Visual C# creates a new folder for your project that is named after the project title, and then displays your new Windows Form, titled Form1 in Designer view. You can switch between this view and Code view at any time by right-clicking the design surface or code window and then clicking View Code or View Designer

The Windows Form you see in Designer view is a visual representation of the window that will open when your application is opened. In Designer view, you can drag various controls from the Toolbox onto the form. These controls are not really "live"; they are just images that are convenient to move around on the form into a precise location.

After you have dropped a control onto the form, Visual C# works behind the scenes to create the code that will cause the real control to be positioned correctly when the program is run. This source code is in a file that is generally nested out of view. You can see this file in Solution Explorer, which is named Form1.designer.cs, if you expand Form1.cs.

If you are in Code view, switch to Designer view by right-clicking the code window and then clicking View Designer. Now change the size of the Windows Form.

Make sure the Properties window is displayed. Its default location is the lower-right section of the IDE, but you can move to another location if you like. The following illustration shows it in the upper-right corner. If you do not see the Properties window, on the View menu, click Properties window. This window lists the properties of the currently selected Windows Form or control, and it's here that you can change the existing values.

- Change the title of the Windows Form.

- Click on the form to select it.

- In the Properties window, scroll down to Text, select the text "Form1," and type "FlappyBird" (that is the name we will use in our code).

- Press ENTER or TAB to move focus from the "Text" text box.

Now we will need to set up our Designer window in order to get started. Head over to the Toolbox section and search for the following things and drag and place them on the form.

- 1x PictureBox

- 1x Button

- 1x Label

- 3x Timer

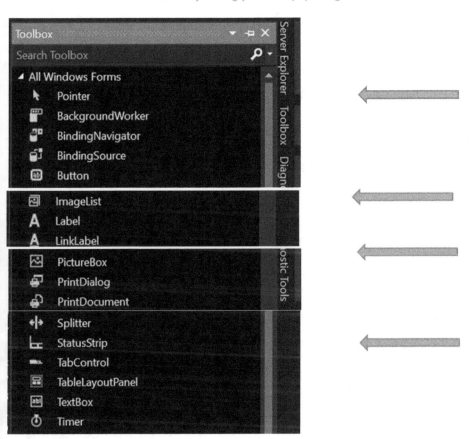

Module - 1: Flabby Bird

Now as we discussed earlier, for each of the tools we placed on the form, head over to the Properties section and change their name for ease of coding.

In reference to the code discussed, the following names have been used for each of the tools we used:

- PictureBox = Bird
- Button = StartButton
- Label = ScoreLabel
- Timer1 = timer1
- Timer2 = timer2
- Timer3 = timer3

Before we start coding, head over to the properties for the StartButton and change the text to "Start". Head over to the properties for ScoreLabel and change the text to "Score". Head over to the properties for timer1, timer2 and timer3 and change their ticks to 1 for each. Then, place the PictureBox towards the top-right corner of the form, this is where our bird will be at the start of the game. Place the StartButton and the ScoreLabel at reasonable positions.

Choose the Bird and assign your image of a bird to it, choose stretch image layout. Resize the bird to about 40x40 pixels in size.

After you have added all the components in your design view, your canvas should look something quite like this (obviously you can use whatever picture you want and i highly recommend you to create your own, so you can develop some skills and creativity)

:

Module - 2: Code

Now let's code. Head to the Code view and add all the namespaces we need. A namespace is designed for providing a way to keep one set of names separate from another.

```
 1 using System;
 2 using System.Collections.Generic;
 3 using System.ComponentModel;
 4 using System.Data;
 5 using System.Drawing;
 6 using System.Linq;
 7 using System.Text;
 8 using System.Windows.Forms;
 9 using System.IO;
10 using System.Reflection;
11 using System.Runtime.InteropServices;
12 using FlappyBird.Properties;
13 using System.Threading;
14 using System.Media;
15
```

The class names declared in one namespace does not conflict with the same class names declared in another. The using keyword is used to tell our compiler what namespaces we are using.

It is not necessary to know what each one of these namespaces does in particular. A namespace usually has hundreds of methods to utilize. After you have added all these namespaces, you will notice that a template that looks something like this will already have been created for you.

```
17 namespace FlappyBird
18 {
19      public partial class Form1 : Form
20      {
21          public Form1()
22          {
23              InitializeComponent();
24          }
25
```

The public keyword in red in the beginning of a method indicates that this method can be called from within this class, or from outside the class. Consider it like an Xbox in your home that not only you have access to, but also anyone who knows that your home exists, also does.

```
26    List<int> Pipe1 = new List<int>();
27    List<int> Pipe2 = new List<int>();
28    int PipeWidth = 55;
29    int PipeDifferenceY = 220;
30    int PipeDifferenceX = 70;
31    bool start = true;
32    bool running;
33    int step = 5;
34    int OriginalX;
35    int OriginalY;
36    bool ResetPipes = false;
37    int Points;
38    int Score;
39    bool inPipe = false;
40    int ScoreDifference;
41
```

Now, let's define some variables (line 26-40). We will be having 2 pipes on the screen at a time, therefore, we create 2 lists and name them Pipe1 and Pipe2 respectively. Next we will define the variables PipeWidth (the width of the pipes in pixels), PipeDifferenceY (the difference between the pipes on Y-axis), PipeDifferenceX (the difference between the pipes on X-axis), start (the game has started), running (the game is running), step (how big of a leap the bird will take on each keypress), OriginalX (the original location on X-axis of the bird at game start), OriginalY (the original location on Y-axis of the bird at game start), ResetPipes (clear the settings of pipes), Points (temporary score), Score (the score of the game), inPipe (the bird is inside the Pipe).

Great, now let's write some functions (What functions? ok sorry). A function allows you to encapsulate a piece of code and call it from other parts of your code. You may very soon run into a situation where you need to repeat a piece of code, from multiple places, and this is where functions come in.

```
41
42        public void Die()
43        {
44            running = false;
45            timer2.Enabled = false;
46            timer3.Enabled = false;
47            StartButton.Visible = true;
48            StartButton.Enabled = true;
49            //ReadShowScore();
50            Points = 0;
51            Bird.Location = new Point(OriginalX, OriginalY);
52            ResetPipes = true;
53            Pipe1.Clear();
54
55        }
56
```

This Die function tells the game that our Flappy Bird has died. The void keyword tells our compiler that this function returns nothing. If our bird dies, we will need to perform a set of instructions. As you can see, the instructions include:

• Setting running to false on line 44, that means the variable that dictates that the game is running is now off.

- Timer2 and Timer3 will be disabled using the timer.enabled

  methods

on line 45 and 46

- The StartButton needs to be visible and enabled when our bird

  dies,

this is set on line 47 and 48

- The temporary score needs to be reset on line 50.

- No matter where our died, we need to take it back to it's

  starting

Position, this is done on line 51

- Pipes are reset on line 52

- The list Pipe1 is cleared.

```
private void StartGame()
{
    ResetPipes = false;
    timer1.Enabled = true;   // timer running
    timer2.Enabled = true;   // timer running
    timer3.Enabled = true;   // timer running
    Random random = new Random();  set a new random variable
    int num = random.Next(40, this.Height - this.PipeDifferenceY);   // random.next(min,max)
    int num1 = num + this.PipeDifferenceY;
    Pipe1.Clear();
    Pipe1.Add(this.Width);
    Pipe1.Add(num);
    Pipe1.Add(this.Width);
    Pipe1.Add(num1);

    num = random.Next(40, this.Height - this.PipeDifferenceY);
    num1 = num + this.PipeDifferenceY;
    Pipe2.Clear();
    Pipe2.Add(this.Width + PipeDifferenceX);
    Pipe2.Add(num);
    Pipe2.Add(this.Width + PipeDifferenceX);
    Pipe2.Add(num1);

    StartButton.Visible = false;
    StartButton.Enabled = false; // disable
    running = true;
    Focus();
}
```

Next, we will write a function that actually starts our game. This StartGame function will basically perform the opposite instructions to that of the Die function. The set of instructions this function will perform are as follows:

- ResetPipes is set to false on line 90.
- Timer1, Timer2 and Timer3 will be enabled using the timer.enabled

methods on line 91,92 and 93.

- We will declare a new random variable on line 194. A random variable is an integer generated by the CPU at run time. The Random class represents a pseudo-random number generator, which is a device that produces a sequence of numbers that meet certain statistical requirements for randomness. We will use this later to randomize the gaps in the pipes.

• Variables num and num1 are the two parts of a pipe. We equate num

to a random variable between 40 and the height of the whole pipe — the difference between the top and bottom. This is defined on line 95 and 96.

• From line 98 to 101 we clear the list Pipe1, and then add the variables

to the list Pipe1, the width of the pipe, num, the width again, num1 in succession

• From line 103 to 109, we repeat the same for Pipe2

• The StartButton needs to be invisible and disabled when our game

starts, this is set on line 111 and 112.

- Setting running to false on line 113, that means the variable that

dictates that the game is running is now on.

- The list Pipe1 is cleared sets input focus to the control.

Now we will head over to the Designer window to set some events. An event in C# is a way for a class to provide notifications to clients of that class when some interesting thing happens to an object. The most familiar use for events is in graphical user interfaces; typically, the classes that represent controls in the interface have events that are notified when the user does something to the control (for example, click a button).

```csharp
private void StartButton_Click(object sender, EventArgs e)
{
    StartGame();  // starts game when button pressed
}

private void timer1_Tick(object sender, EventArgs e)
{
    this.Invalidate(); // refresh, update, invalidate methods
}

private void Form1_Load(object sender, EventArgs e)
{
    OriginalX = Bird.Location.X;  // when form loads set the originalx and originaly to where bird
    OriginalY = Bird.Location.Y;
    if(!File.Exists("Score.ini"))
    {
        File.Create("Score.ini").Dispose();
    }
}
```

If you head over to the designer window and double-click the StartButton, an event that looks something like this will be created on line 117. In this event, we will call the method StartGame. It basically means when you click the button, the function is called and the game starts.

```
private void StartButton_Click(object sender, EventArgs e)
{
    StartGame(); // starts game when button pressed
}

private void timer1_Tick(object sender, EventArgs e)
{
    this.Invalidate(); // refresh, update, invalidate methods
}

private void Form1_Load(object sender, EventArgs e)
{
    OriginalX = Bird.Location.X; // when form loads set the originalx and originaly to where bird
    OriginalY = Bird.Location.Y;
    if(!File.Exists("Score.ini"))
    {
        File.Create("Score.ini").Dispose();
    }
}
```

The next two events are created in the selfsame manner. When you double-click timer1, an event that looks like the one on line 122 will be created. We will use this.invalidate() to refresh the control on every tick*. When you double-click the form itself (the form is the actual window) an event that looks something like this will be created. We will now set the variables OriginalX and OriginalY to the co-ordinates of our Bird on line 129-130.

*Note: Use this.update() if you notice flickering while your game is playing.

In case you noticed, we will use each of the 3 timers to do a specific job. We used timer1 to refresh/update the control every tick. Thus, we will use timer2 to update the pipes. Since the pipes change location on every tick, we will have to write an event for the timer. When you double-click timer2, an event that looks like the one on line 137 will be created. We will now write the logic for the pipes using if-else. Remember each list of Pipe (Pipe1 and Pipe2) has 4 elements. The first condition (line 139) is that if the sum of Pipe1's first element (denoted by Pipe1[0]) and the pipe width is less than 0, or (denoted by the |) the game has begun (start is true) we will fill the list Pipe1 again using the same logic we did in StartGame.

```
136
137 private void timer2_Tick(object sender, EventArgs e)
138 {
139     if(Pipe1[0] + PipeWidth <= 0 | start == true)
140     {
141         Random rnd = new Random();
142         int px = this.Width;
143         int py = rnd.Next(40, (this.Height - PipeDifferenceY));
144         var p2x = px;
145         var p2y = py + PipeDifferenceY;
146         Pipe1.Clear();
147         Pipe1.Add(px);
148         Pipe1.Add(py);
149         Pipe1.Add(p2x);
150         Pipe1.Add(p2y);
151
152     }
153     else
154     {
155         Pipe1[0] = Pipe1[0] - 2;
156         Pipe1[2] = Pipe1[2] - 2;
157     }
158     if (Pipe2[0] + PipeWidth <= 0)
159     {
160         Random rnd = new Random();
161         int px = this.Width;
162         int py = rnd.Next(40, (this.Height - PipeDifferenceY));
163         var p2x = px;
164         var p2y = py + PipeDifferenceY;
165         int[] p1 = { px, py, p2x, p2y };
166         Pipe2.Clear();
167         Pipe2.Add(px);
168         Pipe2.Add(py);
169         Pipe2.Add(p2x);
170         Pipe2.Add(p2y);
171
172     }
173     else
174     {
175         Pipe2[0] = Pipe2[0] - 2;
176         Pipe2[2] = Pipe2[2] - 2;
177     }
178 }
179
```

However, if that condition is not met, we will perform the else (line 153-157), which is to subtract 2 pixels from both the height of the pipes (if you remember the order in which the values were stored in the list) and then continue to test if the other condition is met or not. The second if statement (line 158) concludes that if the sum of Pipe2's first element (denoted by Pipe2[0]) and the pipe width is less than 0, we will fill the list Pipe2 again using the same logic we did in StartGame. Or else, perform the logic in the else statement (line 173). This event is called on every tick made by timer2.

```
private void Form1_Paint(object sender, PaintEventArgs e) // creates pipes
{
    if(!ResetPipes && Pipe1.Any() && Pipe2.Any())
    {
        //Top of the top
        e.Graphics.FillRectangle(Brushes.DarkViolet, new Rectangle(Pipe1[0], 0, PipeWidth, Pipe1[1]));
        e.Graphics.FillRectangle(Brushes.DarkViolet, new Rectangle(Pipe1[0] - 10, Pipe1[3] - PipeDifferenceY, 75, 15)); // length,height

        //First bottom
        e.Graphics.FillRectangle(Brushes.DarkViolet, new Rectangle(Pipe1[2], Pipe1[3], PipeWidth, this.Height - Pipe1[3]));
        e.Graphics.FillRectangle(Brushes.DarkViolet, new Rectangle(Pipe1[2] - 10, Pipe1[3], 75, 15)); // length,height
        //The second from above
        e.Graphics.FillRectangle(Brushes.DarkViolet, new Rectangle(Pipe2[0], 0, PipeWidth, Pipe2[1]));
        e.Graphics.FillRectangle(Brushes.DarkViolet, new Rectangle(Pipe2[0] - 10, Pipe2[3] - PipeDifferenceY, 75, 15)); // length,height
        //Second bottom
        e.Graphics.FillRectangle(Brushes.DarkViolet, new Rectangle(Pipe2[2], Pipe2[3], PipeWidth, this.Height - Pipe2[3]));
        e.Graphics.FillRectangle(Brushes.DarkViolet, new Rectangle(Pipe2[2] - 10, Pipe2[3], 75, 15)); // length,height
    }
}
```

(This picture look kind of blurry so i separate it in 2 below, so you can see it clearly)

```
private void Form1_Paint(object sender, PaintEventArgs
{
    if(!ResetPipes && Pipe1.Any() && Pipe2.Any())
    {
        //Top of the top
        e.Graphics.FillRectangle(Brushes.DarkViolet,
        e.Graphics.FillRectangle(Brushes.DarkViolet,

        //First bottom
        e.Graphics.FillRectangle(Brushes.DarkViolet,
        e.Graphics.FillRectangle(Brushes.DarkViolet,
        //The second from above
        e.Graphics.FillRectangle(Brushes.DarkViolet,
        e.Graphics.FillRectangle(Brushes.DarkViolet,
        //Second bottom
        e.Graphics.FillRectangle(Brushes.DarkViolet,
        e.Graphics.FillRectangle(Brushes.DarkViolet,
    }
}
```

```
179
180  e)  // creates pipes
181
182
183
184
185  new Rectangle(Pipe1[0], 0, PipeWidth, Pipe1[1]));
186  new Rectangle(Pipe1[0] - 10, Pipe1[3] - PipeDifferenceY, 75, 15)); // length,height
187
188
189  new Rectangle(Pipe1[2], Pipe1[3], PipeWidth, this.Height - Pipe1[3]));
190  new Rectangle(Pipe1[2] - 10, Pipe1[3], 75, 15)); // length,height
191
192  new Rectangle(Pipe2[0], 0, PipeWidth, Pipe2[1]));
193  new Rectangle(Pipe2[0] - 10, Pipe2[3] - PipeDifferenceY, 75, 15)); // length,height
194
195  new Rectangle(Pipe2[2], Pipe2[3], PipeWidth, this.Height - Pipe2[3]));
196  new Rectangle(Pipe2[2] - 10, Pipe2[3], 75, 15)); // length,height
197
198
```

Now, we need to create the pipes. We will use the
e.Graphics class to draw objects on screen (line 180-198). In
order to set this event, you will need to go to the designer
window and highlight the form by clicking once on it. Then, head
over to events (a lightning bolt icon) by the properties. Search for
Paint in that list and double-click on that event to create an
automatic definition as we have seen before. Now we will write
the logic inside an if statement. Line 182 states that if the
ResetPipes boolean is set to false and the list Pipe1 has any
elements in it and the list Pipe2 has any elements in it, then run
the set of instructions as follows.

Our logic is based upon the design that there will be 2 pipes visible on screen at any point in time. The two pipes each have two parts, since they are separated by a gap for the bird to pass through. Therefore, we need to draw four different graphics on screen to imitate these pipes.

First we draw the top part of the first pipe, which is going to be a rectangle using FillRectangle, with a narrow base at the bottom. The FillRectangle method takes in two arguments, the color, and the size of the rectangle (length, width). We use Brushes.Color to decide our choice of color we want the pipes to be. In this case, I have chosen dark violet as the color. On line 185, we draw the body of the pipe with the random height we have in the list and the predefined width. For the base on line 186, we declare our size to be 75 pixels wide, and 15 pixels in height.

Next, we will draw the bottom part of the first pipe using the same logic, but this time subtracting the gap needed for the bird to pass through from the end onwards of the top part of the pipe.

We repeat this for the second pipe and our paint event will be ready. Below you can see how the rectangles for pipe1 (the bottom pipe, the bottom pipe's base, the top pipe and the top pipe's base) would appear in the game.

```
200 private void CheckForPoint()
201 {
202     Rectangle rec = Bird.Bounds;
203     Rectangle rec1 = new Rectangle(Pipe1[2] + 20, Pipe1[3] - PipeDifferenceY, 15, PipeDifferenceY);
204     Rectangle rec2 = new Rectangle(Pipe2[2] + 20, Pipe2[3] - PipeDifferenceY, 15, PipeDifferenceY);
205     Rectangle intersect1 = Rectangle.Intersect(rec, rec1);
206     Rectangle intersect2 = Rectangle.Intersect(rec, rec2);
207     if(!ResetPipes | start)
208     {
209         if(intersect1 !=Rectangle.Empty | intersect2 !=Rectangle.Empty)
210         {
211             if(!inPipe)
212             {
213                 Points++;
214                 SoundPlayer sp = new SoundPlayer(FlappyBird.Properties.Resources.sfx_point);
215                 sp.Play();
216                 inPipe = true;
217             }
218         }
219         else
220         {
221             inPipe = false;
222         }
223     }
224 }
```

Now, we write a CheckForPoint function that checks if you earned a point by passing through the gap in the pipes. This time, we create an invisible rectangle object, the size of our bird using bounds on line 202. Then we build two rectangles of the total size of our pipes by initializing a new instance of the Rectangle class with the specified location and size, on line 203-204. Then we build two more rectangles which are defined using the Rectangle.Intersect method, which returns a third Rectangle structure that represents the intersection of two other Rectangle structures. If there is no intersection, an empty Rectangle is returned. These will be the combination of our rectangle that imitates the bird and the rectangle that imitates our pipes 1 and 2 respectively on line 205-206.

The logic behind this move is, if the rectangle of the bird is able to intersect the rectangle pipe, there are only two possibilities:

1. Either the bird hit the pipe, and died
2. Or the bird has crossed through the gap, scoring a point

Thus, if we can make sure that the bird has not hit the pipe and died, it is obvious that the bird crossed through the gap and scored a point.

Our if statement begins with ResetPipes being set to false or start being true (line 207). Then, there is another if-else statement (line 209) that checks whether the rectangle bird is touching the rectangle pipes or not. If it does, we increment Points and play the sound of attaining a point. To play the sound, we first need to initialize a SoundPlayer and then reference it to the sound we want it to play (line 214) Then we set the boolean inPipe to true. Else, we set inPipe to false (line 221).

```
private void CheckForCollision()
{
    Rectangle rec = Bird.Bounds;
    Rectangle rec1 = new Rectangle(Pipe1[0], 0, PipeWidth, Pipe1[1]);
    Rectangle rec2 = new Rectangle(Pipe1[2], Pipe1[3], PipeWidth, this.Height - Pipe1[3]);
    Rectangle rec3 = new Rectangle(Pipe2[0], 0, PipeWidth, Pipe2[1]);
    Rectangle rec4 = new Rectangle(Pipe2[2], Pipe2[3], PipeWidth, this.Height - Pipe2[3]);
    Rectangle intersect1 = Rectangle.Intersect(rec, rec1);
    Rectangle intersect2 = Rectangle.Intersect(rec, rec2);
    Rectangle intersect3 = Rectangle.Intersect(rec, rec3);
    Rectangle intersect4 = Rectangle.Intersect(rec, rec4);

    if(!ResetPipes | start)
    {
        if(intersect1 != Rectangle.Empty | intersect2 != Rectangle.Empty | intersect3 != Rectangle.Empty | intersect4 != Rectangle.Empty)
        {
            SoundPlayer sp = new SoundPlayer(FlappyBird.Properties.Resources.sfx_hit);
            sp.Play();
            Die();
        }
    }
}
```

Again the picture look blurry so i'm i cut it in 2 (read them like they are side by side)

```
private void CheckForCollision()
{
    Rectangle rec = Bird.Bounds;
    Rectangle rec1 = new Rectangle(Pipe1[0], 0, PipeWidth, Pipe1[1]);
    Rectangle rec2 = new Rectangle(Pipe1[2], Pipe1[3], PipeWidth, this.Height - Pipe1[3]);
    Rectangle rec3 = new Rectangle(Pipe2[0], 0, PipeWidth, Pipe2[1]);
    Rectangle rec4 = new Rectangle(Pipe2[2], Pipe2[3], PipeWidth, this.Height - Pipe2[3]);
    Rectangle intersect1 = Rectangle.Intersect(rec, rec1);
    Rectangle intersect2 = Rectangle.Intersect(rec, rec2);
    Rectangle intersect3 = Rectangle.Intersect(rec, rec3);
    Rectangle intersect4 = Rectangle.Intersect(rec, rec4);

    if(!ResetPipes | start)
    {
        if(intersect1 != Rectangle.Empty | intersect2 != Rectangle.Empty | intersect3 !=
        {
            SoundPlayer sp = new SoundPlayer(FlappyBird.Properties.Resources.sfx_hit);
            sp.Play();
            Die();
        }
    }
}
```

```
Rectangle.Empty | intersect4 != Rectangle.Empty)
```

Now we create a CheckForCollision function to test for the first possibility within the logic of the rectangle bird touching the rectangle pipes. We again declare the rectangles the same way we did in CheckForPoint (line 228-236), but this time we have 4 intersection rectangles. If you recall, we divided each pipe into two parts, top and bottom (with a gap in the middle for the bird to pass through). If the rectangle bird intersects with any of these rectangles, it means only thing: the bird has hit the pipe and died.

Our logic for this function is no different. Our if statement begins with ResetPipes being set to false or start being true (line 238). Then, there is another if-else statement (line 240) that checks whether the rectangle bird is touching the rectangle pipe parts or not. If it does, we play the dying sound the same way we did earlier by initializing a new SoundPlayer, and then call the function Die.

```
249 private void Form1_KeyDown(object sender, KeyEventArgs e)
250 {
251     switch(e.KeyCode)  // implemented a switch case statement, case for only SpaceKey
252     {
253         case Keys.Space:
254             step = -4;
255             break;
256     }
257 }
```

Then, we need to set the controls of the game. For that we need to set (you got it!) an event. Head over to the designer view and click on the form, then go to the events and search for KeyDown (occurs when a key is pressed). Double-click on this event to create a definition. Now we will write the logic for the controls using switch-case statements and e.KeyCode.

A switch-case statement is a selection statement that chooses a single switch section to execute from a list of candidates based on a pattern match with the match expression. In our case, we have only one candidate, the Space key. In order for the game to detect you have pressed a specific key, you need to name the key using Keys.Key. Your key could be the spacebar, an arrow, anything.

```
259 private void timer3_Tick(object sender, EventArgs e)
260 {
261     Bird.Location = new Point(Bird.Location.X, Bird.Location.Y + step);   // Logic
262     if(Bird.Location.Y < 0)
263     {
264         Bird.Location = new Point(Bird.Location.X, 0);
265     }
266     if(Bird.Location.Y + Bird.Height > this.ClientSize.Height)
267     {
268         Bird.Location = new Point(Bird.Location.X, this.ClientSize.Height - Bird.Height);
269     }
270     //CheckForCollision();
271     if(running)
272     {
273         CheckForPoint();   // Runs the function
274     }
275     ScoreLabel.Text = Convert.ToString(Points);   // ticker updates the score label
276 }
```

Finally, we need to move the bird across the game according to the user controls. This job is handled by timer3. The logic is to create a new location for the bird on every tick, inclusive with the step that the bird takes on every control, this in motion makes it seem as if the bird is moving. We have three if statements. The first if statement (line 262) checks if the bird is on the floor of the game or lower, that is if the bird's y-axis co-ordinate is less than 0. If so, we want the bird to remain on the floor (line 264). The second if statement (line 266) is that if the bird is on the roof of the game or higher, that is if the bird's y-axis co-ordinate is greater than the height of the form (this.ClientSize.Height). If so, we want the bird to remain on the roof of the game. Lastly, if the game is running (line 271), we want to keep checking for points. So we call the function CheckForPoint (line 273). Also, we need to update the score with how many points we have (line 275). For that we will have to convert the integer value of our points to string to display it on to the screen.

```
private void timer3_Tick(object sender, EventArgs e)
{
    Bird.Location = new Point(Bird.Location.X, Bird.Location.Y + step);  // Logic
    if(Bird.Location.Y < 0)
    {
        Bird.Location = new Point(Bird.Location.X, 0);
    }
    if(Bird.Location.Y + Bird.Height > this.ClientSize.Height)
    {
        Bird.Location = new Point(Bird.Location.X, 0);
        //Bird.Location = new Point(Bird.Location.X, this.ClientSize.Height - Bird.Height);
    }
    //CheckForCollision();
    if(running)
    {
        CheckForPoint();  // Runs the function
    }
    ScoreLabel.Text = Convert.ToString(Points);  // ticker updates the score label
}

private void Form1_KeyUp(object sender, KeyEventArgs e)
{
    switch(e.KeyCode)  // implemented a switch case statement, case for only SpaceKey
    {
        case Keys.Space:
            step = 4;
            break;
    }
}
```

We also want the bird to fall down due to gravity once the key being pressed down is released (Thanks Newton)! For that we will set up a KeyUp event (occurs when key is released) (line 279-287) for the form the same way we set up a KeyDown earlier.

```
    }
}
```

Don't forget to close your extraneous brackets (line 288-289) you have since you started your namespace all the way at the top of your game!

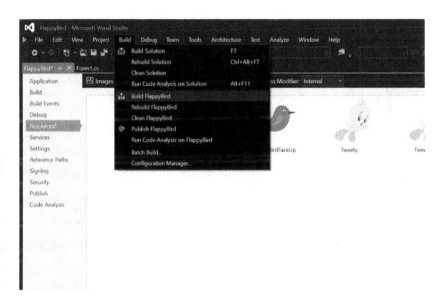

Build your solution by going to Build->Build Solution and... That is it! In hardly 300 lines of code, you have an up and running FlappyBird game you can show off to your friends and family! Enjoy the game!

Module - 3: Make it your own

Ever played a game and thought about fixing something you didn't like? Ever wondered how would it look and feel if you made a particular change? Fantastic! You've come to the right place.. because you are just about to learn how to do that. Let's look at how you can tweak the code in different areas to adjust the game.

1) Changing the width of the pipes

Earlier we saw how to graphically draw the pipes and their bases on the game. We had variables that defined what the width, color, location, and appearance of the pipes would be. If we can define the variables, we can change them as per our choice too!

As you can see, I have changed the pipe width to double its size. And the game feels new and different. But remember, you need to change the size of the bases accordingly! Or else your bases would look unrealistic and out of order.

2) Changing the bird

Remember that the bird is just a placeholder, inside the PictureBox. We can change the bird's appearance, as well as change the bird as a whole whenever we want. Just add the image you would like to use as the bird and add it to the Bird PictureBox.

Below you will see an effect I created using just this property of the PictureBox. As the bird falls down, due to gravity we can replace the image in the PictureBox to change, making it look like the bird is falling

Going up   **Going Down**

3) Changing the steps

Just as the other variables, we set the value for a step. How far the bird will go on each keystroke. If we change that variable, we can alter the speed of the bird as it goes up and down.

Module - 4: Engines and APIs

We used Windows Forms Application to build our game. We can use many other engines and APIs to achieve as we desire. Below is a list of many of such choices out there.

A. Win2D is a Windows Runtime API for immediate mode 2D graphics rendering with GPU acceleration

B. Unity is an all purpose engine, and as a result supports both 2D and 3D graphics, drag and drop functionality and scripting through its 3 custom languages

C. Xenko

D. Anvil

E. Electron ToolSet

F. HeroEngine

G. Visual3D Game Engine is a game engine with a toolset written in C#/.NET for XNA to run on Microsoft Windows and with upcoming Xbox 360 support

H. Torque

Programming in C# is very easy and given proper efforts,

you have the potential to get ahead in an exponential way. C# is extensively used nowadays and later to come. Please practice a lot to get a perfect hold of this programming language and use and contribute on stackover flow and other QA sites.

Signing off. Good Luck! :)

Module - 5: Conclusion

Thank you so much for reading my book, that means a lot to me. At the same time, I would like to remind you to join my email list https://williamrothschild.lpages.co/william-s-rothschild/ to benefit from promotion dates and allow you to be up to date on what I plan. Also did you find this book interesting and educational? Did you notice any gaps in the information given or in its content? If you have a proposal to enable me to improve this book and the next, PLEASE leave me a review. I promise to respond to all comments and act according to your recommendations as quickly as possible. Thank you very much and see you soon!

www.ingramcontent.com/pod-product-compliance
Lightning Source LLC
LaVergne TN
LVHW052125070326
832902LV00038B/3944